THE

LORCA

VARIATIONS

Also by Jerome Rothenberg

JEROME ROTHENBERG

THE
LORCA
VARIATIONS
I-XXXIII

A NEW DIRECTIONS BOOK

Some of these poems have appeared previously in *The Lorca Variations I–VIII* by Jerome Rothenberg (Zasterle Press, Tenerife, Spain, 1990), in a broadside from Ta'wil Publications (Encinitas, California), and in the following magazines: *Below San Onofre, Boletín de la Fundación Federico García Lorca* (Madrid), *Clinamen* (Athens), *Conjunctions, Exquisite Corpse, Notus, Poetry New York, Poetry USA, Le Refuge* (Marseille), *River Styx, Snail's Pace Review, Sulfur,* and *The World.* "In a Time of War" was published as a chapbook by Salient Seedling Press & Diwan (Albuquerque, New Mexico) in 1993.

Manufactured in the United States of America
New Directions Books are printed on acid-free paper.
First published as New Directions Paperbook 771 in 1993
Published simultaneously in Canada by Penguin Books Canada Limited

Library of Congress Cataloging-in-Publication Data
Rothenberg, Jerome, 1931–
The Lorca variations : I–XXXIII / Jerome Rothenberg.
p.   cm.
ISBN 0–8112–1253–X (pbk.)
1. García Lorca, Federico, 1898–1938—Poetry. I. Title.
PS3568.086L67   1993   93–794
811'.54—dc20   CIP

New Directions books are published for James Laughlin
by New Directions Publishing Corporation,
80 Eighth Avenue, New York 10011

CONTENTS

THE LORCA VARIATIONS (I)
"Lorca's Spain: A Homage"

Beginning with olive trees.
                         Shadows.
Beginning with roosters.
                         Crystal.
Beginning with castanets & almonds.
                         Fishes.
This is a homage to Spain.
This mists dogs.
This silences rubber.
This is Saturn.
Beginning with yellow.
                         Eclipse.
Beginning with needles.
                         Insomnia.
Beginning with baskets.
                         The Moon.
Who is naked? The imagination
(wrote Lorca) is seared.
This is a homage to water.
Beginning & end.

THE LORCA VARIATIONS (II)
"Blue Poems/Blue River"

[1]

ivory lips
& blue kisses
trembling:

infinity's river
a branch
a blue apple:

furrows & apples
blue boats
a dead eye:

in blue snow
blue ivory kisses—
a poem in blue

[2]

dream is desire, is
a story
shut down tight,
is old, a blue star

& a little man
inside this unreal
forest, last light
painted

is the earth's, is
roseleaf blue

2

is empty words, a granary
of stars

along death's road,
like memories,
gold worms, a small town
where an army

glides on wings
over its promenades, its
empty benches,
over my heart in blue

a frost my lady
honeyhead will raise a hundred
eyes to, who will seed
new heavens

become a shady form
over the highway
will watch their shells drop
from the other stars

a blue rain covering
lianas
unreal vegetation
& the moon's bald head

blue forehead,
hazy limbs
under a blue sky
now in ruins

Yahweh watching
Yahweh's fir trees, old
& blue, leads forth the virgin
through the mud

[3]

"Coda"

for Jackson Mac Low

lips down words bench lianas	*lorca*
vegetation earth unreal stride longago	*varia*
light snails ivory & so	*tions*
rhythmless like river river river stars	*rivers*
infinite an embedding fills through northern	*inblue*
river river river water river dreams	*rivers*
variations & river ivory &	*varia*
trembling infinity's old new stars	*tions*
in new blue lianas unreal eye	*inblue*

4

THE LORCA VARIATIONS (III)
"Lorca's Clocks"

[1]

A child in
the brambles,
clocks
chiming bells,
one hour,
another runs past.
Love swings from its pendulums,
hanging in clusters
like leaves.
Lorca's clocks
& a bell.
Constellations like clocks.
Two hours
or one
run past death.
They hide in our kisses.
Someone goes cuckoo.
Butterflies dance
on a crankorgan,
blown by our sighs.
A star dreams.
One hour.
Another.
Hours & irises.
Clocks ticking on
in a forest.
Dead.
Black.
New.
Grave.
Pale.

Captive.
Enormous.

[2]

Moons spin like clocks.
Heavy & drowned on
these hills.
Thought becomes murky.
A night calf that dreams about
bats.
Clocks flood dawn.
Summer clocks
spring like a cat
where Oedipus
sighs out his hopes
in a forest.
A spider
seen by a girl
is a sphinx.
Hieratic & savorless.
Bounding the north
is the south.
Winter clocks
in a web
trap her glances.
A clock in a mirror
's a sphere.
Giant swallows fly past,
growing white.

[3]

I & a pool & a ring
make it night.
Time lives in clocks.

As the sphinx
in the stars
lifts stone wings.
An incredible
white.
This clearing means silence.
Stars hide their colors
in sleep.
Time hides in a garden
—bright horns,
a cold roof—
confined to its limits.
Time without silence is
time without night.
A black tower.
Horizons forever.
The damned & their lyrical
butterflies.

[4]

One hour in the forest.
Two.   A pendulum.   Gold bubbles in the air.
Her face & silence.   Three.
In squadrons.   Pocket watches.   Flies in gold.
Gold watches.   O my heart.

THE LORCA VARIATIONS (IV)
"More Clocks"

Hieratic & lilywhite
moons   bats at floodtide
like swallows trapped in a mirror

a sphere like a clock
like your eyes in a spiderweb
girl pursued by a spider

becoming a sphinx at the boundaries
you sit   lady moon
where the dawn knows its winters

you dream   first of nightcalfs & clocks
then of hills   (clocks & spheres
crowd the summer

a cat in a clock   sighing
hoping for oedipus blind
in this forest) whose north is

your south.

THE LORCA VARIATIONS (V)
"Mirror Visions"

[1]

Lantern's rays could be
Lady Moon's mirror.
The hands on that shadow
a man's hands—or someone's,
a butterfly's, everything.

O moon of a child (hosanna!)
& visions in mirrors.
A glowworm. A quicksilver
heart. A blue jesus.
Lantern's rays could be everything.

[2]

Their eyes that were roses
are crystal.
Their god is the air.

His arms pull birds
from a mirror,
scatter lilies over the dead.

He turns swans into stars.
A cloud rises over the earth
like his replica.

[3]

"Capriccio"

Twilight's mirror holds the image of a blank young
    mummy.
In a baby book the sunset breaks the wellspring's silence,
    aie!
Does a star hide in her flesh? the dew reveal its light in
    mirrors?
In its nest a mirror sleeps. The mother's echo cracks its
    shell.
Rainbow brilliant let us fly forever among the desiccated
    dead.

[4]

"Shinto Eyes"

Shinto eyes.
Shinto ivy.

    •

Irises tinkling.
Real forests.

    •

If teardrops are roads,
fields are death.

    •

Eyes like flowers.
A castle. A fountain.

10

·

Pagodas a boy watches.
Traveler with bells.

·

God alive in a ricefield.
Herons over the road.

·

Red virgin. A crossroads.
Pinkcolored garden.

·

A woman casts shadows,
lights up our eyes.

·

This emerging volcano,
this fountain with dragons.

·

Golden & primal,
endless, horizonless,

·

God in a necktie
stares out

thru two secret eyes.

[5]

adam	eve	serpent	mirror
pieces	apple	rock	sleep
mirror	sleep	fear	eye
sleep	butterfly	word	light
keyhole	sleep	heart	mirror
garden	love	kiss	lips

[6]

Air keyed to
heart,
like passion to crossroads,
or sunsets to owl.

A firefly feeds meditations,
old rainbows
dear to your heart,
as clothes gather slime.

Meditations in swarms.
Cold star in a mirror
is mirroring
him, you, myself.

He's a brother. His people
wear glasses.
An owl flies over the grove.
Show me color.

Thoughts. Everything
hands have a hold of—
or hearts.
Show me sighs that glide downhill

on wings.

THE LORCA VARIATIONS (VI)
"At Night"

[1]

A blue man
walking down a road
goes home

past crawfish, past
a stable
in the forest:

there his eyes see
fir trees, see
old people moving

see a weevil: bullocks
sound a prelude,
a new star

above the mountains
that he sees
along his road:

a crawfish slowly
turning eyes,
a night he paints

with fireflies,
grown bleary
like a weevil, blue

with sleep, with
starheat,
rising

through the night.

[2]

Windstars, the eyelids'
milkyway caresses—
it's a bird, magnolia-
colored, 's set in
hut or hand, again
the eyelids shut on it,
again the starlight
brings a lemon,
yellow painted roses
flicker, paint your forehead
with a star,
the water splashes blue,
the pond where love
joins star & tree—
romantic, crazy
starroads
lead me,
I am frog & star,
again, again,
in tranquil space.

[3]

Bear belly
like a lady's—
she is mother star,
is tender, loony
moon, whose babies
suck a ring
grunt
grunt
is stars inside of
stars inside
a wheel.

[4]

"Poor stars" or
"poorhouse" stars
(she names them)

their blue light right for
lamentation   Venus
at night among lianas

tight with sorrow—
as when a comet kicks up mud
—cries open sesame,

but space falls on her,
her sorrow ghosts,
sorrows rise past Sirius,

her days are dark with
stars, a harp that carries
lamentation   sorrow

to her babes, that cries
shut sesame, reflects a sound
she hears down labyrinths

of poorhouse stars.

[5]

Sadness that comes with
light
while night looks down on
ocean, on the earth,
casts tiny tendrils.

THE LORCA VARIATIONS (VII)
"Water"

for Charles Bernstein

[1]

Under the spring
a silver tremor—
as of oxen trampling
daisies,

memory a lake,
a dead tree floating
on the mountain water

mind & heart
a single highway here,
dark tree in middle of
a black field

nightingales & poppies
hurtling home.

[2]

The moon drops flowers in your hand.
A widow, waiting in the dark, escapes you.
Only a little tamer than the universe.

.

Only a single stem on this acacia.
From it you pluck a star & butterflies.
Here in your night my heart is dark.

16

•

Here the roots curve inside your night.
You who would look so blue.
Here is a way for love among the stars.

•

Only acacias, water lilies, love.
Tamer than my thousand years along this path.
Here make your way into the infinite.

[3]

Glass beehive.

Other moon cells,
this gateway
for my kiss.

O crystal prison,
o beehive
made of air!

THE LORCA VARIATIONS (VIII)
"Backwaters"

See him in ice & in pain
(mad Lorca)
see him in cypresses.
Dead in his eye,
in his tongue.
Stagnant water lies over him.
Poplars cut deep
& glass willows.
Water is locked in his heart.
In his eyeballs.
Dead air.
Metal branches.

THE LORCA VARIATIONS (IX)
"A Cuckoo Suite"

[1]

Cuckoo who echoes cuckoo's
whistle,
who floats like cat's tail
over space
like bird's foot fox can read
as symbol:
wind in the pines,
night's pellets dropping
from bird's beak,
its centuries split open
showing cuckoo
adrift in sailboat,
swan uplifted
into lady's thoughts,
o cuckoo whispered through
our copper lips,
our home beset by flies
who echo cuckoo
voices   by that girl
who flaunts a fox-
tail, taunts
desires, like eternity,
bright pellets that a child might drop,
there where a cat eats time,
a magpie is a sphinx,
who laughs the day away,
reveals
a cricket nesting
in a crystal,
in words that echo
Lorca's words.

[2]

Night's end is on this ground,
where Noah touches Noah.
Time falls down.
Time gets to grow a beard.
The farm stays good & empty.
Here I sing a song.
He did sing of siglos & the sky.
Methusaleh will sing Methusaleh,
will make us *cuckoo*.
Siglos & whistles will be launched.
The hombre in the ark's
asleep & old.
Amen.

[3]

Enduring,
the soul is a wind
& endures.

It gets lost in the night
first cuckoo escapes from.

The sobbing endures,
the eyes, being lost,
crave its smell.

Down in the canebrake, uncertain,
nocturne loses its power.

Cuckoo falls down.
Cuckoo gets lost.
Cuckoo loses his bucket.

20

[4]

(The night.
The waterdrops.
No no.)

(An angel winds his clock down.)

(Last resurrection for the cuckoo.)

Goldfinch singing yes,
his confines open.

(Night says no
inside its garden.)

Eye says yes yes.

(Flowers line gate down which
a second cuckoo
dribbles.)

(Nocturnes.
Time.)

[5]

When day shudders,
oceans & towns
float off.
Is it my love?
the cuckoo thinks
& sighs,
sees daggers,
says this town is clean
but bitter,
o my love,

my love,
your shuddering is cuckoo's
sigh,
is oleander,
moon & olive grove's
last nocturne.

THE LORCA VARIATIONS (X)
"Sublunar Visions"

[1]

blue stars
like infinity's moons,
bells on moon

so distant,
the sun like a heart
lost from sight

faint bubbles faint memories,
moon & earth
crossing at moonrise,

blue perfumes,
islands & oceans,
dim paths to the moon.

[2]

is moon the moon of deserts?
spiderweb moon or a violet moon
over cities? the dead moon of legends?
a white moon? the moon cracked & soundless?
lost in small towns? a stainedglass moon
shining on graves? reflecting all colors?
a green moon? the moon over Paris?
a true moon of color

[3]

moon & star
& the chrysalis moon   sublime
in her frantic word *evening*

who is lady at sunset
breeds stars
spider's sisters, o sunset

sunset   gold   black
o Salome   palace of kisses
moon & Salome

this beautiful chrysalis,
sleep,
like Salome   Medusa

like moon o Salome Salome
o sky that moon's fixed to leave,
moon crying thru mouth

thru lips, darkest desert
with shadowy smoke   a cocoon
for her soul   night & day

water trembling, moon
with the head of the moon
& love in her eyes

is moon's endless story

THE LORCA VARIATIONS (XI)
"Newton"

[1]

The men had green feet that vaulted them into the open where they could flaunt their secrets. Lace brushed lightly against their nostrils as the apple tree loomed over Newton with its fruits. It is so Saxon to bind gnomes with string, to watch your echoes drifting off in secret, your lost companions jangling irons in the wind. Not every boy has such sad eyebrows, nor would every corner spare an inch for death. In the woods the moon showed Newton where the truth lies. Following his nose he slammed into a meteor named Newton. He mistook it for a science that was white—like beech trees or like beards—but once he caught it in his mirror, saw it turn blue again. At length it looked like every other star or lake.

[2]

Every wise man considers himself another Newton: a philosopher musing beside trees & water, going for a walk or coming from a walk, pulling genies out of waves & sky (with which *sigh* makes a perfect rhyme). Their corneas are focused on infinity & disregard the lowly cricket just as Newton did. And just as Newton knew the wind or Wordsworth knew a certain road to be the night's reflection, so apples floating on a wave of crickets make a synthesis more powerful than stars. Philosophers should play guitars, then, reaching for those apple branches where the moon's a lowly apple. Pyramids adorned with owls express a kind of harmony; & stars are dots & are a proof of death more powerful than worms. What if the river strikes a pose? the cedar will show a face that brings it home.

[3]

There isn't a clue that the fruit into which Adam bit was an apple & not his lady's breast. Above them Pegasus kept flying past, all in the name of science. The Virgin handed him a second apple, which Adam turned into a questioning of history. Deep in its core the Virgin saw souls rise & fall: a symbol Newton later found inside a pomegranate. Only a child can play with apples & touch beauty; Newton & Adam both were satisfied with Eve's reply, the first she gave when she woke up in chains, her innocence laid by. Paris in the other tale held up an orange.

THE LORCA VARIATIONS (XII)
"Federico, Newton, Adam"

[1]

Federico in Paris writing about Newton's soul without a
clue to what it is.

Federico bites into a pippin, rotten to the core, the symbol
of himself as Adam.

Federico with an orange & a pomegranate that the Virgin
hands him from a bowl of fruit.

With his childlike innocence Federico raises age-old ques-
tions of the meaning of the apple.

Federico in the chains of history compares his apples to a
pair of breasts.

The first truth Federico gets to see is Beauty's, the second is
a Pegasus dressed up as Science.

Federico & Newton stand next to Adam & Eve. The Virgin
hands Adam an apple & they all await Federico's reply.

[2]

Federico makes the pyramids his home as long as there are
apples left to eat.

Three owls visit Federico in the night & greet him as the
wise man in the cedars.

Federico discovers Newton's face reflected on the moon.

Federico standing on the road is posing with an apple & a
glass of water.

Where the river branches Federico waits with Wordsworth
like a pair of old philosophers.

Federico spots a worm in his apple & a wind in his trees.

Federico takes Newton for a walk & hears Death plucking a
guitar.

Federico thinks his walk with Newton is proof that he's a
philosopher.

Federico hears the sighs of genies & the crickets in the stars.

Federico conceives a synthesis in which infinity & waves
become a single dot.

Federico's cornea sees stars & crickets covering the sky.

Federico thinks the sighs the waves make teach him har-
mony & rhyme.

[3]

Federico is sailing on the lake just as a wind comes up.

A green star lodges in Federico's eyebrows, which amazes
his companions.

Federico repaints the Blue Boy with a pair of iron feet.

Federico moves two mirrors from their secret corner & sets
them in the open.

Federico delivers the men with beards to Death, then listens for their echoes.

Federico wanders through the woods, where gnomes in beechtrees are exchanging secrets.

Beneath a perfectly white moon Federico flutters strings of lace.

Federico hears Newton breathing science through his Saxon nostrils.

Riding on a meteor Federico spots the truth beneath a fruit tree.

Taking the apple Newton hands him, Federico shoves it under Newton's nose.

THE LORCA VARIATIONS (XIII)
"Fireworks Suite"

[1]

grenade in god's night
where you singe
my hair   you call me
"poet"
a barrage of light
so green it lights me
who am not me
am not you   who dream
a birthday for us both
with fireworks
first little poem
you launch for me
a wheel of fire
I burn into your forehead
down your earlocks
a gold star I hand you
who are me or you
no longer   floods with light
this shadowy occasion when
we're born & die

[2]

the mystery of how a sunflower is all a sunflower can be
is all a providence that sees its peoples in a sunflower
a disc inside the eyeball
like a sunflower that covers all
the way an eyelid covers all an eyeball sees

& yet the lens seeing the heart sees nothing
but the fair fills up with abels
shuddering & swooning
gazes aimed against the heart like ruby arrows
a stigmata hovering above the savage crowd
sans irony
much as a cyclops winks

[3]

a gardenette implanted with small teeth rain dripping
down like commas on its blue magnesiums   night falls &
torches a guitar   screens hide a girl whose cherryos &
fuming purples puff up sparkadillos in her bell jars
chsssssssssssss   the night sky shines under our fingernails
dragondolas alive like zigzag babes the wind drives through
its woodlets   if saint george appears & spears a mouselet
then the mirrorettes beneath would hurtle skyward   or-
anges besiege the princessitas' gardens   golden serpents
spurt up fumes like rockets

[4]

Ziiip Zaaap Ziiip

if the peacock
was love

then this girl would grow
feathers

& this hombre would also
grow feathers

& their eyes would grow eyes
ziiip zaaap ziiip

[5]

the moon is afloat in a ring
it drifts
with its own dead torrents & swarms
as a moon it is gold
like the moon on a treadmill or the moon on the ocean
light striking a fountain of moons
moon's a loaf we cut into
a waterwheel lifting a moon past your window
climbing the sky with a cane
we see petals & leaves on a moonwheel
a screen hiding the moon from the moon
& more moons & more fountains
as bright as mirrors in which our eyes play:
a game of black crystals

THE LORCA VARIATIONS (XIV)
"Wheel of Fortune"

for Diane Wakoski

[1]

fan-tan is a game of chance,
as risky in the present as the snake who finds a little
    girl,
or as a zodiac in red,
a star in green,
a yellow sky from which a bird pulls numbers,
four five seven,
twenty fingers count the numbers in this forest,
& the little girl with four eyes printed on her fan cries
    "yes" & "no,"
before she glides past—wet & smiling—on her wheel
    of fortune

[2]

blind peacock,
eyes like pinballs, cold,
like fake corollas,
tail devoid of flesh

toward which her hands move,
clear across the garden,
she plucks jewels
from among the roses

grand inquisitor
who smears the sky with
numbers, staking out a game
of blurred roulette

THE LORCA VARIATIONS (XV)
"Water Jets"

[1]

If death once had a face
the water from this water jet
has wiped it out,
the August air has left no trace of it,
like other fountains
or other faces from your home town
that the sunlight & the water jet
drive from your room.
Things leave our eyes no boundaries here
other than dreams, no dreams
still precious to your heart,
its carved interior shot through with corners,
into which a grapevine grows,
fed by the water jet your fingers
once turned on, made it a place of clouds,
the perfect death's head still inside it,
& that a water jet wipes out.

[2]

It's night.
In the garden our hearts have turned blue.
A maid opens the water jet, lets water & roses spill out.
A century passes.
Pianos circle the earth, dark swords slice arteries.
No dust on your windows, just blood.
In the garden four gay caballeros trade swords.
A cloud breaks apart & starts quaking.
It's night.

34

THE LORCA VARIATIONS (XVI)
"Seaside, Sirens, Stars"

for Sargon Tont

[1]

The Directions

Drop a lid down on the cavern's mouth,
or daub a column with gold scales,
from capital to capital,

the sea will suck the gold into its gullet,
leaving the summer ripe for contemplation,
the water sliding down your shoulders,

sea in rapture,
sea with lances raised,
songs fit for giants,

like an old print of pines above the sea,
of coral sirens preening at the seaside.

[2]

The Personages

Mary is sitting in a tower, seated in a kingdom
ruled by Polyphemus, odors arising from her water-
    drops
until they touch the stars, or where the stars

cast shadows, Christopher is sitting in a second tower,
watching for daybreak, awaiting Mary in the daybreak,
welcoming the guards for whom the earth's a heart,

its oceans alive with stars, the odors from the stars
empowering the guards, those rovers proud of their
    own
features, who find a second vagabond astride the sea,

Venus arising from a nucleus, a waterdrop,
to stammer a new nocturne, wailing,
where she will still come to be.

THE LORCA VARIATIONS (XVII)
"God, Dark, with Palm Trees"

[1]

Mediterranean sky.

With flowers sprung from his arms,
Zoroaster is riding the wind.

(Call the sky Zoroaster.)

He who floats on an octopus,
shading the palm trees,
he who shines like a star.

Mediterranean water.

A palm tree hanging in space,
its limits are Satan.

A rose that shines like a star
& Satan riding
an octopus,
vibrating.
Shading the palm trees.

[2]

A palm tree rears up from the sea.

The Graces haul salt from the country.

Gorgon's tears,
& the Mediterranean's
shifting its sands.

With contemplative rhythms,
with negresses drifting in silence,
with olives like iodine.

Shake your feet.

A spider & stork in a pine tree.

Dates on palms
turning blue,
waves growing rusty with iodine.

Disentangling your hairdo.

[3]
Fat patron,
chewing olives,
where the sea
is rhythm always

sea on top of sea,
blind Peter
with his whitewashed
omphalos

beneath the heat
that Jesus Christ gives off,
transforming seas
to deserts

its sailors showing Aphrodite
penises like columns
with crowned capitals—
blind seas

that cannot see their own waves
striking poses
at the sky,
o towers overblown with sound.

[4]

Blue wheat
Eve sifts with her hands,

or a lemon
borne by the river.

What grace,
oh what gold's in the air

leaves us swooning:
a palm

is a palm
is a palm

at whose summit
yellows appear,

they rear up in curves
over these palm trees.

THE LORCA VARIATIONS (XVIII)
"Those Who Wait"

[1]

When dawn rises from the prairie in Chicago,
tremors destroy a spiderweb in Spain.

When an arm's cut off from its fingers in Chicago,
plows push the clouds across a field in Spain.

When shadows hide signs along the river in Chicago,
roosters start sifting through the chaff in Spain.

When an umbilicus dangles from a body in Chicago,
glowworms rise up from a soul in Spain.

When a house smells of flesh & burning in Chicago,
the ocean swells with rivers flowing out of Spain.

When lanterns illuminate a broken body in Chicago,
lanterns wash away the shadows of a nose in Spain.

[2]

Spanish eyes, the secret of
façades, of sun above
a ridge, a Spanish geyser,

the Chicago river, both the same
at sundown, x-rays
in the air,

the twilight set in bondage,
of hens in Spain, your words
move past the heart

into the gut, they find
the shadow of some stars,
always the same,

a sphere encases us,
we trudge a sinister ravine,
a sundown in Chicago,

rooms explode their glass,
a rooster, dreaming, dreams us,
displacing those who wait.

THE LORCA VARIATIONS (XIX)
"In a Time of War"

[1]

Snuffed out in mind
or heart
the war sucks up the dew,
dries out the spring,
the water thickens,
daisies wilt,
a stone drops through
a dark lake,
near a silver mountain,
nightingales
lie dead,
a tremor uproots three
black trees,
uproots the memory
of trees
& oxen,
the poppies from another war,
another homeland.

[2]

War makes a prisonhouse a thousand cells crisscross in: a
universe we enter down a single road.

[3]

A widow in the darkness gathers roots the slender stem of
an acacia curving in the love she brings a love that floats like
butterflies over the road to war.

[4]

Inside the glass a crystal moon lives war will shatter into flowers in the endless night.

[5]

Once the night grew tamer once the stars destroyed by war inside their hive fled to the open air.

[6]

Moon acacia water lily star: even a year of war won't hide or tame them.

[7]

War waiting in the gateway to the hive.

THE LORCA VARIATIONS (XX)
"Songs at Nightfall"

[1]

Lorca's Granada
turns white,
like earth & its nightingales.

Trees with the sound
of a bell,
shore losing its green,
rising up.

Sunrays mask
the horizon.

Soul's in its boat
where fishermen,
shadowy moles,
snag fishes from fishhooks.

Sad brunette,
little leftover heart,
old willow
lost among fishes.

The soul beats a drum
in time to the sun.

At nightfall
the mist
brings us songs,
dreams bring us sorrows.

A pond shines with
silver lianas—
cypress trees
under the moon.

[2]

Whites in the field
play at wolves
(pianissimo) bagging a bird
in the poplars,
tying a lamb's feet.
It's evening,
the blues running wild,
lordy lordy,
distances bringing delirium,
shoulders down deep
in the river, too much!
(pianissimo) gold
of the evening
& gold of the bee-eaters,
arms drawing landscapes
from silence, from dark
(pianissimo) gold (pianissimo)
solitaire.

[3]

The dead climb a stalk to the sky
    do-re-mi
The moon holds a glass for her lover
    do-re-fa
Her husband with a rose sings an aire
    do-re-mi
& the briars on the prairie have turned white
    do-re-fa

A memento of poplars bright as chalk
    do-re-mi
& a funeral with the dead bearing snakes
    do-re-fa
A distant ocean & cold towers in the night
    do-re-mi
whose stone bells sound deeper than the sky
    do-re-fa
In her heart there's a mountain blue as night
    do-re-mi
Mad poplars & a bonfire by a streambed
    do-re-fa
A confusion of glass birds & of the wind
    do-re-mi
Deeper deeper & more distant than a star
    do-re-fa

THE LORCA VARIATIONS (XXI)
"The Return"

[1]

To write through Lorca, to come back on Lorca's wings, to return to where you're feeling empty, like dying sweetly after love, to where a rose has left you wounded, the shadow of your childhood like a flower inside your heart, where Lorca's road trails off into a garden, in which the morning star drops colors onto a faded dress, like paint.

[2]

To come back on Lorca's wings, who sees his origin in water, sees his soul die in a dream, transform into a corazón forever, sees a shadow overwhelm the flower in his heart and cry goodbye, until his soul returns to him, a muddy spot from which a butterfly arises, shivering, a gust of wind in motion through his heart.

[3]

To see his origin in water, in the dawn, a feeble sight, the motion of her corazón, of Lorca's wings in water, making love down at the oxbow, hearing the nightingales, a love as sweet as perfume, goodbyes & reminiscences turned into songs, a girl & a muchacho turning & returning through the spray.

[4]

To return with Lorca only yesterday, to walk along the sea, under the stars, to see the forests becoming green forever, green with love, the shadow of our childhood like a flower, crying adios! while marching single file up to a crossroads, reciting the songs we made, white muslin shaking, trailing along the byways, the glitter that drops down from Lorca's wings, words that we write through Lorca.

THE LORCA VARIATIONS (XXII)
"Shadows"

[1]
Midsummer.

Night sky hides
the earth.

A tower hides a roof.

Wind splits the sky up
into many skies.

Shots slam against
the stones,
& birds dive down
from roofs.

The sky erupts with memories
when daybreak looms.

The sky drifts by in series.

[2]
The echo of the dead clears up the mystery of ghosts.

Therefore life smells like yeast. It is a lamp that lights the
world at night. The day's elixir.

He is the owner of the sky. He sits in judgment. His heel
looks awesome in the shadows. Everything you ever loved
turns into ruins.

The desert at its ends bristles with stars like bats. The night
brings four ships filled with silver.

We have witnessed the demise of wilderness, he said, the
end of love.

We have lately seen a bat become a star, we answered.

[3]

He who watches from the roof, sees
poor old bulls who vanish
in that blackness,

feels their sadness when they pull
his white cart,
they are like his horses,

dragging stars across the sky
for seven days
or two,

gold horses & a toy cart
on the road at night,
poor old driver plodding sadly

under ursa major.

[4]

A mountaintop.
A flock.

There's Saint Sebastian
shaking in the breeze.

Clouds hide the stars.
Buttes hold the night.

My heart takes wing.
A tinted violet grows cold.

A mountaintop.
A shepherd.

A crystal mountaintop
with shadows.

Desire for camellias.
Depths of sky.

Grey sundown.
Sunset over highways.

Eros shredded.
Rusted in the rain.

[5]

Vespers lingering.

Exquisite eyes across
a gulf of colors.

From its branches
tears hang.

Shades conceal the highway.

Jeremiah waits
& gestures.

(Gestures.)

Jeremiah sobs.

A willow stops
existing.

51

THE LORCA VARIATIONS (XXIII)
"White"

Proem. Days dissolve. The ink inside the album starts to fade. Constantinople turning white erases Eloisa Lopez. And that archbishop, really something else. See where she's got him in her album—what indulgence, oh my soul! He's like a little white thing.

[1]

First White

Birds fly down
from the moon

in white March
(open sesame!)

white & unreal
like a child

on the prairie
a flower

(open sesame!)
white in the forest

a cherrytree's
shadow.

[2]

Second White

Frost on her feathers
is white.

Moon's also white,
& white kisses

grow cold on the syrinx.
Dead Leda,

her flesh glowing white
in the forest,

& Pan, sailing by
in his boat.

When it's night
the blond swan,

golden cygnus,
throws open his wings.

[3]

Third White

White's a conjure for clouds
& for mountains
with the clouds on their shoulders.

Stars are conjures for wings
& for snow
where stars drop down from the clouds.

Mountains are conjures for stars,
for all white conjurations.

[4]

Fourth White

Snow across the fields reveals the cock's crest.

•

Stars still shine at dawn.

•

The cock's crest suits him like a blouse.

•

Stripped down he greets the day.

•

A first laugh drives the stars away.

•

His gold crest soon turns white.

[5]

Final White

There were "romantic" words to end with—"tree" or
"house" (or "treehouse")—before he got into another

"novel." March was as sharp as "vinegar" & there were some longhaired "schoolboys" writing "verses." Did they notice how white a "thing" the "snowbird" was when they saw it after "school?" Also that "basil" would grow best in "sand"—that "love" could be "sweet" as "cherries," not like "vinegar?" With Eloisa "dead," there was a "grandmother" who sewed her "lips" shut. That made a "springtime" for "dead" Eloisa, with her "name" lit up by "candles," and "girls" who looked like "baby dolls" blowing "white feathers" toward her. O little "rose" inside your "convent," said another, bring a "bottle" for the "dead" down to their "boat." "Mockorange" is the little "secret" we perpetually write out.

THE LORCA VARIATIONS (XXIV)
"Lorca's Mirror"

[1]

look thru this lens,
she told him,
& pressed it hard against
her sex

& so he did,
to watch it through her mists,
he who was Lorca,
was the boy who wore a necklace

a silver boy among
the gold muchachas—
searched for her
under a wounded sky

heard her call him
little heartthrob,
streaked across the sky to her,
to be her star

like someone riding from Venezia,
astride his pony,
with star dust trailing after him,
a lyrical narcissus

Federico wrapped in pearls,
who struts before a mirror   sees
the sky reflected in his lens—
a renaissance of silver boys

[2]

never content until you
hold a rainbow pillow,
until the child inside you
comes alive

& you grow boobs,
dear Federico,
your altered body hides the sky,
tied to it by the tail

a sky with sliding shadows,
railings set up in front,
the stars kept back—
the way it would look in prints

you pour through & you see
three lovers sleeping
in the night, the ocean
tight around them

& know that one of them will be
your little hearthrob—
he with his tophat gleaming
in your mirror

you emerging from its waters,
Venus newly born,
curved neck & trembling hand
tracing her shape

THE LORCA VARIATIONS (XXV)
"Two Allegories"

[1]

Meditation & Allegory of Water

A Jew went dancing with the wind. It pulled him in concentric circles—grew cold enough to change his soul to crystal. Trembling, like a clutch of hidden Jews, the sheep bells rang at sunset. Were the birds there truly wind birds? Immense perspectives past the reeds & poplar groves. The surface of the water teemed with eyes. Drawn to that spot, the wind tore down a dark enormous flower. The Jew was quavering. His skin was bright with stars, his heart was yearning for the golden strands of sunset, lights reflected through a prism. As the days turned green, he noticed other Jews among the brambles. Spiky osiers pointed skywards from the pool where bee-eaters flew by in summer. Venus, atop a waterfall, could see the Jew's soul taking flight, his body light as leaves. A rounded mobile greenness. He is a smalltime dreamer, yet his afternoons are spent in counting gold. Perched in a treetop one whole afternoon, he soon disturbs the crystal with his silent stirrings. On another afternoon he hangs a cloth up in a tree & leaves it there for coolness. Waves rush up the avenues and down his throat. Algae engulf his soul—for years he dwells beside the river, like a cicada by the water's edge. Nearby the air winds in & out between the solomonic columns, revealing phantom nuns with birds in place of hair. The Jew recalls a trip, where drops fall down, where echoes rise. Small memories of Jews & violins.

58

Along the Border

Summer in the desert.

A Jew goes in search of gold but finds only dead bodies. He hangs a cane over his arm, then races down the valley in his Ford. Blue desert music follows him—crazy arabesques & dried fish out of Nowhere. *How long before I reach the olive groves?* he wonders. And asks himself: *what current drives my Ford?* How white with gold the sand is & how blue the sky. The olive groves are heavy with cicadas, the trees with yellow ribbons, & waves of people, still fingering their flutes, flow past in silence. Souls dressed as birds hover over the road, their lights invisible, like water in the desert. *I felt a clove of garlic brush my face,* the Jew says. *It was like a fragrant curve. A waning blue moon risen from the depths.* Fantastic algae block him from the rear. His ear against the road, the long road, measures the entire valley. But no one can tell its boundaries even so, although they race around it in their Fords. So might a frog be lost at sea, then. And someday, if November comes for them, the olives will release their taste, the crickets desert the valley. A young boy, with his forgotten dreams of mountains, hangs antennas in the poplars. He will be waiting on the road, until the Jew approaches, smiling, with a green man's head & oh what spiritual eyes! They will drive off in his Ford, down through the valley that now reminds them of the moon— yellow air choked off with yellow ashes, air & river thick with garlic, whirlpools spinning backwards, so much confusion in their ears. Cut off from home, they watch a line of men along the road, close by the border. Gold is pervasive here. And contradictions. A clash of musics. Sounds of desert & of ocean. Cemeteries, fishtanks. Song arising from the music all night through. Night arising from the desert.

THE LORCA VARIATIONS (XXVI)
"Palimpsests"

[1]

It stands there, written, for them all to see.

The forest that is here today will disappear tomorrow. The warriors will rush into the oak grove, down a living corridor, the blue monks scattering around them.

Two by two the hapless gentlemen will enter, they will squander gold like air inside a ruined city.

Houses overturned. The sky above us looped in an enormous curve. A white sky hidden by the sky at night.

Two gentlemen disguised as hunters, wrapped in mauve. Two other gentlemen disguised as gentlemen.

The boughs inside the forest shine like crystal arrows. In a city underneath the sea the sky is living coral. Corridors stretch out for all to see.

The sky beneath us hides another sky. A white sky hides inside a sky of gold.

[2]

all sounds constrict
into a scream,
all signs into a spiral

in whose wake
its many rhythms change
to yellow

words & birds
so painful,
they leave a thousand scars behind

the air dissolving
in their wake,
a whirligig set spinning

turning black

[3]

somewhere like wax smeared on
an oak tree   adolescence
runs from us from you
who show your breasts to me in april
covered by my hands

sweet girl not in granada
but in the bronx
those towers that hide a girl & not
a woman   not a spindle
that she holds

but something fecund
ripe with branches   reaching
from my heart to yours
some lucy growing red beneath
a full moon

stares down from her towers
until a half moon rises
lifting up her arms
to dance   her hands lit by the moon
by bonfires

eve she is who waits here
snowwhite breasts
my hands press down upon & cover

& my foot moves gently over hers
awakening a madrigal

etched into wax

[4]

this fountain
fountain
where the birds drift

this sky
the oranges fall under
like a sky

this fountain
fountain
where the corn is green

this corn beneath
this sky
this sky inscribed

on this last page

THE LORCA VARIATIONS (XXVII)
"Lorca's Journals"

Six Songs at Nightfall

6/22. Arrived back in Granada, feeling a little wild & lonely. Earth was funny (white) today . . . nightingales, trees, whatever else we looked at. A bell was sounding from a distant shore, horizon alight with pale green sunrays. The soul sets off now in its drunken boat, the fishermen dig underground like moles. I watch them dangle fish from fishhooks, each with a brunette in his heart . . . a fresh green willow to haul in the fish . . . a drum to call the soul back. Every time the sun goes down it's nightfall, & every time the moon drops in the pond, the lianas & the cypresses turn silver. We endure with sorrows old as dreams . . . as shadowy as mist. Forsaken, solitary in the dark, I write *Six Songs at Nightfall*.

A Voyage to the Moon

Last night my heart had snakes in it. I was dead & taken to my funeral, from which I climbed up to the sky, like climbing up a stalk, to find the dead awake & walking on the moon. The moon was made of glass in which I saw my lover growing cold beside the ocean. Mountains reflected in the streambed shine like towers, & the poplars wind up in the bonfire. It's a night of stone bells—out there where Rosa's husband breathes the prairie air. White briars. Distant sky. Confusion of winds & stars. Blue birds have drawn a face across the sky, as poplars have. The chalk you gave me scribbles a memento.

Water Jets [1]

The water jets are broken & the maids haven't been in to clean. Something dark broke through the garden in the night. My heart is useless, in which my arteries ran wild & banged like pianos. Dirty centuries & dirty water. Blood drips from a rose, it smears my window, covers the dust piled on my sword. The world's a garden complete with swords & caballeros. Night starts in again behind a single cloud.

Water Jets [2]

Waking from a dream I touched death with my finger as he fled from me, but couldn't see his face. The water jets were pouring all around us, every room wet down to the darkest corner. It was as far from August as from home, as far from sunlight as from clouds. And still the air was throbbing with its water jets, fountains as heavy as my heart, a place where things can disappear without a trace, like dreams, like water from a water jet. Later your face comes back to me; interior boundaries dissolve; a grapevine trembles; a water jet's deflected by your eye.

Zoroaster

—Admit it, Zoroaster, you're no star.

Satan turned back & looked at him, then turned back twice & looked again.

In fact he looked a little like an octopus.

—Who did?

Satan, the way he stood in space, his arms stretched out beyond the sky, refracted like a palm tree in the water, like a rose, a flower drawn up by the wind & planted gently in the Mediterranean.

—This one has no limits.

64

But a palm tree by the Mediterranean is just another palm tree.

—Admit it, Zoroaster, you're no star.

—Fuck you, you lousy octopus.

The Double Agent

After the second siren blew he left the capital & drove down to the seaside. There were two caverns visible beneath the water, a scene remembered from old prints. A pair of scales was floating on the sea, & the sea itself reflected coral & a splash of summer gold. Softly a song came toward him from the sea, reminding him of giants sleeping, those massive columns that rose up now like lonely pines. Why fight the sea, he thought, or hack away at it with lances? If he could just put a lid on what he saw & banish contemplation, the sea might vanish by itself & the capital would be restored. But the thought of it weighed heavy on his shoulders, shaking him through & through, then sticking in his gullet.

A Master Builder

"The city will be located wherever you would like it. (All this is up to you.) Its streets will look like zigzags—to match your way of thinking—but viewed from overhead will more resemble intertwined ellipses. Rooftops will be as high as cypresses & will be covered with dry grass. The towers we build will all have porticos, & the men & women walking through them will sport rare feathers pasted to their foreheads. We will most likely call the city Babel—or we will go through all your poems until we find some other word to name it."

—You must be moon crazy (said a man).

—Oh yes, I love the moon so much, I'd race across it on a treadmill.

—And yet a moon is best defined by eyes. We stare around it cautiously, like looking through two mirrors in a single light.

—Or with the moon as light, we turn aside, we turn aside & end up in a mirror.

—Shine the moon down on the screen, it gets the sky & all reflected.

—Surround the moon with crystals. Then repeat what's here.

—[He reads.] *A leaf is not a loaf. A wheel is not a waterwheel. A moon is not an empty mirror.*

—There's a ring around the moon, then. When we look at it like that it turns to torrents. It is now an ocean.

—In it stands a fountain. Several fountains, come to think of it.

—From the window swarms of peacocks fly across the moon. A gilded peacock glides in front of you & drops gold feathers.

—Play a game of moons to end it. Walk beneath the moon &, leaning on your cane, pick up her shining feathers. String them up like petals fallen from the moon, until the moon drops down to where you wait & buries you.

THE LORCA VARIATIONS (XXVIII)
"For Turtles"

[1]

Up there—or down here
for that matter—the screams
rush around us
Ellipses dismember the tower
of Babel, crapulent city,
enraged zigzag women still sit in
with feathers, on porticos
Men with pale foreheads
shout poems from its rooftops,
crushing its grasses,
city that's buried in words,
like "cypress" & "daylight"
"up there" & "down here"

[2]

My heart is flying from me
—see it fly—
& rising in a spiral,
like a star,
a spiral rising past the Cape
obliquely,
like a neon heart,
celestial turtle set before the pope,
until the turtle & the star
drop back to earth,
to test the limits of a heart,
the way that hunger
tests the soul
or feet whatever life is left us

A heart, a soul, & many turtles,
where the heart transforms
the body, like some pluvial
sahara, & the turtles
blot out the horizon,
leaving turtleshells & wings behind,
unto our final rest

THE LORCA VARIATIONS (XXIX)
"Lunar Grapefruits"

Prelude. Mirror of a country night. Pale blue letters & a cross to match our feelings. Do they reveal a wall or cover up a sword? Do we appear pretenders to each other, rust disfiguring a garden or common sense occulting evil? There's a feeling still—of creatures hidden in the underbrush, a man whose life is only pain, a state he struggles with & that destroys him. Tree leaves fall like doubts & words like flowers; my face is painted silver & my clothing too. Along this dark escarpment, see the clouds roll in— says someone—& hear the frogs depart. We are making preparations for our white museum; we will name it for Don Carlos, & when it turns to yellow we will change its name. Later we will fight the dragon so that good may triumph, & our eyes will look through glasses (ultraviolet) to glimpse the future. Rivers will turn the waterwheels beneath our house & towers will rise above it. Something like a piece of wood will drop into a jar or will be pinned to my lapel (it will protect me on my journey). Here is my satchel—see!—& here a page that's open to reveal a nightingale. A man is shown surrounded by concentric circles, & the snake we see here symbolizes war as would a sword. Your enemy lies dead under this poplar, where little things like eyes are stippled on him. When we drive down to the prairie there's a hidden wall at first & then there's fruit; otherwise no landscape you could speak of. A family is hauling buckets through the dawn, decked out in lace & praying to the Lord. Exotic roses & a sprig of cherrywood are on my nightstand, where I count the time it takes to move through time, the kind of costume that it takes to win repose. Invisible, ecstatic, we are making blueprints for our death, are plotting points between the garden & the orchard, opening a hieratic landscape. Is it so wrong to fight our feelings, to convert them to a phosphorescent white, a reverence for grandfathers who crowd into our rooms & make a subtle sound like wings in motion? Multiplied until they're endless, they are walking from your balcony into the sky, their scent is omnipresent in the dawn, & they are waving at you like a tribe of friends.

[1]

> [Question]: Do the wings really matter, or the way a gryphon-bird swoops down upon a child?
>
> [Answer]: The search goes on in the old folk tale. Near the portico a dwarf is talking to a child.

The Dwarf
I was shrivelled, having set out on a quest to find the living Virgin.

The Child
Earth rang out. Clang-clang. You stood under the stars & trembled.

The Dwarf
Hoes hacked at *me*. A single plane flew by & scraped the pinetrees.

The Child
Sea & moon were weirdly motionless. You killed what I-You-He had made.

The Dwarf
I was uprisen now. I mingled air & earth.

The Child
On your walk you felt the earth beneath you tremble.

The Dwarf
I heard it sounding in the shadows. Clang-clang was how it
spoke.

[2]

Huge mouth with
yellow smiles
with no one's laughter heard
among the leaves,

among the moons
circling above this forest
by whose doors
your smile was waiting,

like a smile that someone's
always spitting up, a door
that's always jamming—
grapefruits whirling overhead,

your laughter taking wing,
escaping through your teeth,
like Adam's, crammed in that first
forest, nailing skulls

over its doors.

[3]

A tower of milk.
Blind domes
& boredom.
Night river lost in my beard.
Clang-clang.
Sapless poplars.
Crowds setting sail.
Grey water.
A spasm convulses the earth.
Blue lights
& a wind snake
shine forth.
The century vanishes.
Leadeyed.
Lead eyeballs.
Stiff branches.
The moon is an eggshell.
Perennial.
Old situation.
Old man.
Old birds at a catboat.
Old river.
Clang-clang.
The sky turning blacker
than flesh.
The atmosphere hectic.
Paved over.
The light drawing back
from us others.

[4]

He dreams of flowers,
foliage that holds his soul
like crystal,

sparkling,
& walking from a turquoise house,
cling clang,
a garden in the distance
& a key,
light years away,
he smiles a smile
a child might,
who mimics gold inside
a yellow dream,
cling clang,
his eyes like ancient discs
not like those grey souls,
those greyer shadows,
sleeping in a crystal house,
alone & trembling, swinging
horsewhips underneath
a christmas moon,
its bells struck motionless,
cling clang,
his lips alive with
butterflies,
a hundred swords at rest,
ah, while he smiles
& buggers you,
now spawns a key of frost,
cling clang,
a star he hides,
misguided,
screaming heehaws from
his tower, seeing
crippled halfmoons rising,
sharp as spikenard,
bridges in the mud,
& staring without eyelids
from his world house,
water grown that vast

& heavy,
now encircling him,
a beggar,
cut off from his world,
the dragon year
beginning
in his eyes, a forest
everywhere
in which a skeleton is waiting
with a crown,
another with a diving mask,
cling clang,
the bells inside his garden
gone, the light bells
floating,
bringing his words to birth
at christmas,
in a dream of rivers,
his shoulders now the only props
against that worm,
old worm that rises on old wings,
lives with him inside
a white house, crying
adios, & adios
again, old yellow beard
in tatters,
high atop his tower.

THE LORCA VARIATIONS (XXX)
"Jewish Cemetery" (1)

Daylight like hospitals
where corpses burn   where gloves
are cast aside
the women's anguish buried deeper
than our hearts, the children
crying in that fire
like a million herons, children
who have lost their way,
hang here from ropes
with pains down to their feet
& blood that spurts out
from their eyes   cut through
by scissors

.

It is girls & doves who fly here,
Christ who guards this prison,
who hides this gate   Christ's
joy & fevers
see—they say—that dove
there in the center
no bigger than a hummingbird
& see it leap!   it flies
over your walls
like Christ   good pheasant
ah! good doctor,
crouches at your table
who wears a surgeon's coat
beckons the buried dead
with brightness

Ah! how his chrome does shine,
lights up the martyred landscape,
chastely,
offers his death to all—
locusts & jews alike—
he drops hot lead into your water,
blights your lettuces,
your ships he shakes with fevers
& your cemeteries, nightly
with his forsaken jews

THE LORCA VARIATIONS (XXXI)
"Jewish Cemetery" (2)

Let them cover her eyes with rags when the dusk begins to
 gnaw her joints
& let the donkeys pass her by let them crack down hard
 against the marble
& let the fevers cut across her like a claw
or a boot assault her with the terrors Jews feel in their
 cemeteries

Let her set out on boats the way the Jews set out on boats
 who sought an entrance
when everything turned blue dissolved in blackness moans
 so loud they drowned the lyres out
& fear slid down the slopes & left its footprints in the mar-
 ble

Let her heart escape its port her children sleep in boats like
 splintered galleries
where clocks are bound by chains & blood drops from the
 moon to stain our columns
a body rigid in the desert dry & hard a Jew with open
 mouth whose moans are lost
children who carry sunflowers of cardboard specialists have
 cut for them nocturnal ribbons flying from our domes
like doves the rain falls down on underneath our wheels
 where Christ grinds down his Jews

And let the waters rise against the gangways let the Jews
 still sit in silence watch the dew turn white in autumn
 with its frost
& let the architecture vanish under leaves like ancient der-
 bies buried in the grass & let the air blow through our
 gates piled up with snow

no man will walk here & no visitors will fill our beds no
    doves will rise above no caterpillars dig below
no nightingales will sing with joy no names will comfort him
    or her squeezed out between green teeth
will find a cemetery trembling hands of Christ will break
    through she will watch her Jews through rags & eyes

THE LORCA VARIATIONS (XXXII)
"First New York Poem"

[1]

Science & the paradise of labor give hope to those who live with anguish, whose dawns are buried under mud.

·

The challenge arises in my blood. It brings me games to play with bones till morning ends it—spikenard afloat on water, columns swaying like a distant shipwreck.

[2]

We control the children's noises with our laws, their mouths distorted into mindless angles.

·

Above New York four pigeons—silhouetted, black—fly from your fire escapes, but no one sees them.

[3]

Numbers we write down clank like drills or chains.

·

Impossible to know your boroughs any longer, to recall the dawns that struck New York with hurricanes, rattled coins, that let love die before it blossomed, spattered your rootless crowds with faded light.

THE LORCA VARIATIONS (XXXIII)
"Second New York Poem"

> El mascarón. Mirad el mascarón
> cómo viene del Africa a New York.
> (F.G.L.)

[1]

"They Are Gone, the Pepper Trees"

Half of it was sand
    & what remained
        was mercury & made him
tremble,
    too afraid to rub it in
        while visioning
a hippopotamus who stalked through
    everlastings,
        & other animals who crossed
those endless bridges,
    whom he could bring down
        with a spear,
their beaks grown dormant,
    their flesh nailed onto trees
        from which he used to cut his masks,
would wear his masks around
    New York, half crazy
        wasn't he,
the bright gazelle mask flashing
    where he walked,
        what joy to be among you
at this gathering,
    he thought,
        to spend this time with you
here where the wheat rots,

swans rut, camels
            plod among the peppers,
in the mask that shows you fear,
        the mask dissolving into sand,
like solitude & ashes
        where the light has died away
                so recently,
the cat is playing with a cork,
        & all things come into this other light
                the phosphorous ignites
over New York, where death
        's a crocodile, & sunlight
                makes the world
grow darker, where a sword cuts through
        my throat, my feet,
                where silence covers everything,
where eyes turn white,
        where time turns inside out
                like valleys
rife with mutilated buds
        in Africa,
                inviting us to join
their dance of death.

[2]

"Canyons of Lime Imprisoned"

A fond farewell
        at the border. See the dead
                & how they hunker down,
who bring us hurricanes,
        those naked masks,
                those shameless tumulters,
who tempt us with strange lights
        horses will ride past,

81 of course, 81

          slender mounts for children,
edging their way through niches,
     squeezing
               into bank vaults,
Wall Street poor & empty,
     roofs on which manometers
               break into pieces,
& the channels they leave behind
     excite the iris,
               yes, & voices
cut across New York, & someone
     wears a mask
               that looks like North America,
& someone else counts up
     the unemployed, whose numbers
               brought together in a frozen dance,
o Lorca,
     darken the sky.
               These herds are what we will become,
their frenzy
     will be ours tomorrow,
               o my naked heart,
we watch the sphinx together,
     squatting inside this cemtery,
               she with a bank director's mask
& you a chinaman's,
     your profiles soon identical
               except that you
still sing your deep song
     while the sky fills up
               with down, & fireflies
grow faint & then invisible.
     Time hides
               inside you, can you feel it?
does it press against your mask?
     whose groans
               are rising in this place?

whose blood is on our blueprints
　　　even now?
　　　　　　is there a formula to chart
the impetus we feel? a yellow thread
　　　to recollect it?
　　　　　　　when I dance, the naked wife says,
it is no less for money,
　　　when I give you tail
　　　　　　you fade in me & die,
the stillness
　　　overtakes you, sky
　　　　　　is split asunder,
lime & mire splatter on the snow,
　　　the night makes even gold
　　　　　　turn black for us
who wait here at our windows,
　　　watch old columns
　　　　　　lit by flames,
the impetus returning
　　　like a wheel that spins
　　　　　　forever
in an empty bank vault,
　　　see it with your own eyes,
　　　　　　hear it cross this space
in silence,
　　　watch her naked body
　　　　　　in your mirrors,
feel the sap press upward,
　　　as if moving among mountains,
　　　　　　guano everywhere,
to drown in guano,
　　　living,
　　　　　　buried in its canyons.

3

"I Was on the Terrace, Wrestling with the Moon"

Below us, men in iron masks
    who rob a bank,
        lie buried in a landscape
with the dead,
    fear dripping from them,
        seeds of light
under our windows,
    where those who pass us groan
        like swarms of cattle,
press against store windows
    that reflect the sky first,
        then the blood that spurts up
when you bite an apple
    sweetly, sweetly
        when the dancers mass around us,
others dressed like shepherds
    crying silver tears,
        cold earthworms,
standing on streetcorners in the dawn,
    near where the young girl
        rises from the flames,
still others whom you couldn't know
    cut off her hands with broken shells,
        the tiny drops igniting
in the air,
    smear yolks between her thighs,
        & beat the moon
with oars, as I do
    wrestling on this ancient terrace,
        watch me, watch me,
whose eyes blaze in the night like stars,
    who gaze down Broadway
        like a prairie,

I who offer up a mollusk
        for the dead,
                slam virulent guitars
against my thighs,
        who wait with Lorca on a fire escape,
                a pyramid behind us
to welcome our forgotten king & pope.

[4]

"'Don't Let the Pope Dance!' Someone Cries"

"Don't let the Pope dance!"
        someone cries,
                "El mascarón. Mirad
el mascarón."
        It's Lorca crying,
                Lorca coughing poison
over Wall Street, dreaming
        of a courtyard
                covered with blue mosses,
of sodomites in masks,
        cathedrals where frail millionaires
                adore a King,
where dancers drift around
        like madmen,
                scorched by scarlet fever,
stung by nettles,
        & it's Lorca perched atop
                his pyramid, it's Lorca
smuggling rifles through the forest,
        Lorca in the mask of anguish,
                trapped in vines,
or Lorca in the stock exchange,
        the floor collapsing under him,
                it's Lorca in a mask with emeralds

for teeth, a mask
    to charm the Pope back to New York,
        to wear in jungles,
to stare out of on terraces,
    a mask with cobras that the builders
        have forsaken,
the Pope has jammed over his own,
    not dancing, no,
        but turning blue,
cries out with Lorca
    for the mask,
        it's Lorca's mask
we wear together now,
    el mascarón,
        he cries to us,
the mask! the mask!

CODA: THE FINAL LORCA VARIATION

the end for Lorca comes
only when we let it   helpless
with insomnia
we hear him stir   we see him
reach for Saturn
rising overhead

no homage can repay what we have lost
our false beginnings   naked crystals
bathed in the imagination
needles that sting us, rubber
that brings us down
a rooster who cries against his shadow

where it still smells of almonds
dogs are howling
at the moon   eclipses in the water
olive trees for Spain
& castanets
our homages stuffed into yellow baskets

offered to Lorca's Spain

A POSTFACE TO *THE LORCA VARIATIONS*

I was recently involved in an extensive Lorca translation work, which brought me full circle to the first translations I ever attempted: some Lorca *romances* worked out and never published, when I was still in my teens back in the later 1940s. It was shortly after first word had come to me of Lorca, circa 1947, from Tom Riggs, who was my brother's English teacher at NYU. I was fifteen at the time, and Lorca had been dead for some eleven years—nearly three-quarters of my life. Time of course seemed longer then.

Lorca for me was the first poet to open my mind to the contemporary poetry of Europe and of something possibly older and deeper that would surface for us later in America as well. Reading his poetry then, the words & what they seemed to fuse in combination hit me like electric charges. *Romances, coplas, gacelas, casidas, llantos*: old forms that came together in old/new patterns to make what he/they called a *cante hondo* (deep song). Or "The Lament for the Death of a Bullfighter," with its repetitive tollings & its flow of deep images. And the final discovery of all that that might lead to in *Poet in New York*: for me a first entry to surrealism & the crucified marvelous (the crucified word-&-image of a Dada poet such as Hugo Ball) as it erupted, beyond recognition, in a city that we thought we knew.

Lorca was the first, and it was from Lorca more than anyone else that I brought away the idea of a composition through images (through charged conjunctions & disjunctions) that I later named "deep image." By that naming—circa 1960—I found myself positioned between poets like Robert Kelly & Diane Wakoski on the one hand, James Wright & Robert Bly on the other. The field of course had opened by then beyond Lorca and in Lorca's work itself had moved from image as such to what Lorca in one of the great examples of a twentieth-century poetics had called *duende*. As an *active* poetics—opening like Antonin Artaud's theater-of-cruelty to ideas of possession, of struggle, of those "black sounds" that make of art "a power, not a construct"—this concept of *duende* as an "earth-force" made of Lorca a major precursor for the revolutions in poetry & life erupting again in the 1950s. (His political and, as we were to find out later, *sexual* martyrdom at the hands of Spanish fascists contributed to this too.) Entering into that maelstrom, then, I found that Lorca's glamor had similarly touched poets like Jack Spicer, Robert Duncan, Paul Blackburn, Amiri Baraka, Allen Ginsberg, Robert Creeley, among the many I was soon to meet—a whole generation in fact, not easily bounded by even those groupings with which I later sensed myself to share a common cause. Blackburn it was who defined our search as one for an "American *duende.*"

Time has not diminished Lorca for me in that sense, though it has clearly set his work against that of a wide range of other poets, other poetries, works that in their vastness seemed at some point to open nearly limitless possibilities for our modern & "post"modernist concerns with language & reality. With all the changes from his time to ours, Lorca has remained a beacon—a poet, as I read him, who can be rediscovered & can turn out differently at each point of recovery. A number of years ago, coming across a series of scattered & early poems of his called "*suites* [Suites]," they struck me as a different kind of Lorca from what I had known before—still characteristically his but with a coolness & (sometimes) quirkiness, a playfulness of mind & music, that I found instantly attractive. The full run of his Suites—first brought together & published posthumously in the 1980s—shows other Lorca characteristics as well, but my attempt, as far as I could, was to stress the more playful ones, as if to pay homage by so doing to this most graceful & elegant of twentieth-century poets.

Beyond the Suites, however, which were commissioned as part of a large collected Lorca translated by a variety of hands, I felt a frustration in not being able to publish my own translations independently, thus diluting whatever sense I had of doing a Lorca homage, etc. With that in mind, I began to compose a series of poems of my own ("variations") that draw on vocabulary, especially nouns & adjectives, from my translations of the Suites (later from *Poet in New York* as well) but rearrange them in a variety of ways. I don't know how important this information is for a reading of the poems, but I mention it to explain the way in which these poems both are & aren't mine, both are & aren't Lorca. The methods used resemble chance operations but with a margin of flexibility, with total freedom in the case of verbs & adverbs, with occasional addresses to Lorca himself imbedded in them. The result isn't translation or imitation in any narrow sense, but yet another way of making poetry—& for me at least, a way of coming full circle into a discovery that began with Lorca and for which he has stood with certain others as a guide and constant fellow-traveler.

Jerome Rothenberg
Encinitas, California
1992/1993